A Fulfilled Life:

The Key To Your Happiness
and
Professional Success

Commitment

How serious are you about having a loving and happy life?

Many people say they are, but very few are deeply committed to this outcome. On one level we all want it, but on another level we want it only if there is no hurt or pain caused by bringing up old emotional imprinting and negative issues.

Making a commitment to enjoy a happy life requires that you let go of most of what you know to be true in your current beliefs and conditioning. This is a very scary thing to do. All sense of security can be washed away, and quite often one can feel very vulnerable, exposed, confronted or even isolated as a result of taking this step.

It is not all doom and gloom, however, as I am here to tell you that the greatest joy one can experience is waiting for you right now. On the other side of the deluded perceptions, resistance, insecurity, the unknown and fear is a treasure chest of all the joyful and loving jewels you seek.

All that you seek as a human actually resides within.

Located in your heart space resides a divine doorway that leads to all the joy and happiness that most people are struggling to find and attain. The key to divine consciousness is waiting for you right now in your heart. It is this consciousness that brings to you all of your dreams.

Pure unpolluted truth, which is all knowing and loving, desires and is willing to bring your life into a loving and positive state that only dreams are made of.

Sustained happiness — which is what all humans' desire — is not something that is found outside of you. All positive experiences happen because of your alignment to the divine energy that is held within you. It cannot be found anywhere else.

So the commitment required to allow the beauty of divine happiness and love to unfold is the commitment **YOU** make to **YOURSELF**.

It is the commitment to make the decision to step through the consciousness doorway in your heart.

It means you will not listen to your ego and mind driving you to stay right where you are — in your delusionary past conditioning and beliefs. Nor listen to the ego/mind telling you that you don't deserve happiness, or you are not valuable or good enough to succeed.

It is the commitment that **YOU** accept what drives and motivates you to seek the divine within; trusting your soul's consciousness always has your best interests at heart.

It's your trusting that its connection to the almighty power of God/Consciousness has a divine plan for you, and you will never be able to stray from its unfoldment.

It's the commitment to allowing yourself to feel safe in trusting Divine Plan.

Sometimes you may think your life is all over the place and you are not where you think you should be. However, this is only your distorted view of truth appearing as real and giving you a sense of disharmony, struggle or stagnation.

Your commitment is that you *keep alert* to not falling into old patterns of non-truth and negativity. Put concerted effort into always aligning yourself to positive spiritual truth and don't support non-truth within yourself or others.

Are you prepared to put that much effort into changing your life?

Are you prepared to embrace your truth, warts and all?

Are you prepared to make a difference in your life regardless of what it might take?

Do you feel you deserve or are valuable enough to have a happy life?

Are you prepared to let go of all that prevents you from seeing truth?

These are all very valid questions to consider if you are really serious about changing your life. Your commitment is very black and white: you are either committed to happiness or you are not. There are no half measures or room to be blasé.

Making a commitment to grow towards more happiness requires that you let go of the myths you hold within your beliefs and perceptions; myths you currently think to be true.

It requires that you always express how you feel in all situations; that you remain vigilant and aware in every moment, so you never ever repress your thoughts, feelings and emotions.

It means you must be fully open and allow your life to unfold without any interference. Just let yourself 'be' in your divineness.

A commitment means you choose to perceive and know all experience as positive in the bigger scheme of things. You always look for ways to support your life with loving thoughts and actions and your interactions with others.

This is the commitment that is required if you wish to truly enjoy a good life.

This is the commitment and effort required to truly love yourself.

You are driving the bus of your life. Only you hold the controls to brake, accelerate, to turn left or right.

Which way do you wish to steer your life?

The choice is, and has always been, yours to make regardless if you feel otherwise.

The time has never been better than right now for you to make the changes necessary to bring you into a life full of joy, ease and abundance. It only requires that you make a decision to do so and to commit action to it.

Practice

Find yourself a quiet place and sit and consider the following:

- Am I worthy of having a good life? Answer: Yes

- I am a divine fragment of God/Consciousness.

- My soul made a decision before I was born to consciously lower its vibration and awareness, to limit itself so it could experience this limitation and all that it brings. It did this to make all things in existence even more complete by having direct experience. With experience comes more wisdom.

  This process is how creation grows and advances. This was something very special your soul has done, and it should be honoured. One of the ways of doing this is to live a life in alignment to spiritual truth and spiritual ways, to do your best to not hinder your natural unfoldment.

- I value and love myself, acknowledging the divine pure being who I am.

Make a decision to do whatever it takes to value and love yourself right now.

Decide to be alert to what you are creating in any given moment, and if it is negative, do your best to positively change.

Sit now and deeply consider these things.

The Purpose of Human Incarnation

Why are we here?

This would have to be the age-old question everyone would like answered.

When one understands the true reason why we are here one's whole outlook on life is changed. Life is seen through new eyes, without distortion or cloudiness.

Contrary to popular belief, we are not here to get married, have children, work and save to buy a house and to live happily ever after. Some will do this, some won't; however, there is a bigger and more profound reason for existing as a human. There is a divine reason for our existence on this amazing place we call Earth.

To start with, we need to look at the big picture from the perspective of universal truth. Science and the universe both tell us that all things in existence are made up of energy. To take this one step further, all of this energy is actually a part of the one field or greater whole.

Call this energy what you like: *Prana*, *Life force*, *Universal Consciousness* or even *God*. The truth remains that there is a divine force and consciousness that permeates everything in existence.

When we pull back the veil that has been holding us in an illusion created by our negatively conditioned minds we can see there is no such thing as separation — all things are, and have always been, connected and are as one. The experience of the illusion of separation appears real because we live in a vibrational realm that has duality.

We are all just little segments of the whole interacting in our own little unique ways — this is a Universal Truth. Through this interaction with each other — in fact, with *everything* that exists — we colour in and create all together an amazing vibrational picture of existence. So, in effect, what you do in any given moment impacts on the whole.

Our true purpose within this whole is to actively play a part in fulfilling the consciousness of the universe and beyond by attracting to ourselves unique experiences. Depending on how we react or respond to these experiences, we can alter the nature of the vibrational whole. As we change, so does everything else. Through the changes we make, we paint another stroke of colour onto the big picture.

Isn't it amazing to realise this?

To take this one step further, this is how God/Consciousness (or whatever label you wish to give the divine whole) is able to have direct experience and continually evolve. For simplicity's sake, I will just call this energy *God*. (If you do not believe in such concepts just substitute *God* with another label.)

We are in a sense a little piece of God (a God-fragment) having experiences available in this reality to fulfil the greater aspect of God's intention to create. This really is our sole purpose and the reason for our soul to exist in this reality. If we happen to get married, have children and have a happy life, well, that is a bonus.

Knowing that you are a piece of God changes everything. You no longer see yourself as separate or exclusive from everything else. This goes a long way to changing how you perceive and interact with people. Everyone is actually a part of you.

So, if you value God or anything or anyone at all in your life you have to also value yourself, as there is no difference between you and them. Part of your commitment to a fulfilled life is that you value and love 'all of you', 'you' being everything in existence.

Have you ever heard of the old saying "as above, so below"?

God is above, yet God is below in every piece of creation. There is actually no difference between God above (that amazing beautiful energy or creature) and the God-fragments below (you and all life), except for their current vibrational state.

The innate nature of the lower existing fragments of God is exactly the same as God above. As each fragment of God broke away from the bigger piece and descended down into the different realms of reality, their level of frequency became more solid and dense.

As each fragment dropped in vibration, it experienced a decreased awareness of itself and of the higher realms of vibration. Each God-fragment became unaware of who it actually was.

The denser the energy, the less the smaller God-fragments (us!) see. This decreases each fragment's ability to access the understanding and abilities of the bigger God and its intention to create. Life was created this way to allow us to experience negatives, as the bigger piece of God desires an experience of all types of energy, and it does this through its God-fragments! In the process, all is enriched.

A good thing to remember in your dealings with other people is to remember you are interacting with another piece of yourself — God/Consciousness. Being hurtful, critical or negative in any way toward others really affects the quality of your life. Remember, you are energetically a part of all life; there is no separate self — that is an illusion.

In a broader, more spiritual sense, you are the people you meet.

A good question to keep in mind is: "How much do I love and value *myself*?" In other words, in my interactions with others, how much I love and value them is directly related to how much I love and value myself.

Practice

Pondering exercise

Pondering is a wonderful technique to become more aware of that which someone is pondering on. It makes the particular thing more present or real within a person's conscious reality.

Pondering, sometimes called *daydreaming*, is an easy process of putting one's attention and focus onto what one wishes to ponder. Don't grasp, judge or control the pondered subject. Just gently, without effort, give attention to the subject and allow your mind to be free. Every now and then, if your mind floats too far away from the original subject of your ponderings, gently come back.

Ponder the statements below, one at a time.

- My purpose is to gather energetic experience to make the bigger part of me (God/Higher Consciousness) more enriched and fulfilled.

- God's intention to create manifests throughout all life. All experiences I attract to myself, and how I respond or react to them, serve this purpose.

- All experiences, people, places and things have the same value in the bigger scheme of things; there is no need for judgement.

- It does not matter what anyone does. They are just another part of my/the whole's gathering experiences; this is exactly what I am doing.

  - I am energetically linked to all life, so what I do to others I am in fact doing to myself. Separation is an illusion of duality.

  - Everything is equal and a part of me.

Sit now and deeply ponder...

All Creation is the Same

All of God's creation has the same value and purpose.

Where equality exists, judgement has no place.

All of creation is doing the same thing — having direct experience of energy. All animals, plants and insects, even the planet itself, are gatherers of energy experience for the whole.

There is a belief among many people that we are here to present lessons to ourselves. In the bigger picture this is not true. When you truly realise why you are here you will understand there are **no lessons, only experience gathering**. This is important to remember; you are just a gatherer of experiences. That's it.

However, by evolving in our human consciousness through spiritual practice and gaining understanding and knowledge through our day-to-day experiences, we raise our frequency. And in so doing, we are opening up another level of potential experiences available on Earth.

As we rise in frequency through greater understanding and clarity, we make choices that allow our life experiences to become more happy and joyful. This can appear as learning, and in the narrow sense of the word it could be called that. However, in the big picture it is just a transition from one experience into another.

This is the process of experience gathering, which enriches all life. By moving us through experiences created via the Law of Attraction, we are able to access all of the broad-spectrum energy and information available in this vibrational reality we call Earth.

No judgement of better/worse, good/bad is placed on individual experience, as all experience is serving the same positive purpose — to allow God to create. Life as a human, like all life, is in a constant state of change from one experience to another; this is creation in action.

We are only here to be gatherers of these energetic experiences, to play our part in creation.

A key point to remember

Even though we are living in a reality with a multitude of energies, some positive and others perceived as negative, we can move through all experiences with love and joy. It was not God's intention for anyone (a piece of itself) to suffer. It is, and has always been, our mind and its conditioning that makes experience gathering a burden. When negative experience is seen as just more experience to gather for the whole it no longer burdens.

By becoming detached, trusting Divine Plan and seeing all experience as having the purpose of *experience gathering*, we can have a happy and contented life.

Another thing to think about here is that every person alive is doing the same thing. Sure, we are all doing different things in life and are attracting different experiences, but in the big picture it all serves the same purpose.

Equality exists in all life and experiences.

Recognising and taking on this understanding to be true — that all of our experience gathering is serving the same higher purpose — goes a long way towards removing the burden of judgment from your life.

You should be truly grateful for what every other person does in their lives, whether you perceive it as positive or negative, as this is making you, as a fragment of the whole, more complete as well. Understanding this will help you to see all interaction with other people in a totally different light. Each and every one of us is helping each other.

Isn't this absolutely amazing?!

When you truly see what purpose you are playing in the divine plan you will totally change the way you perceive your life. By knowing that all experiences, and the gathering of them, are of equal value in the big picture, you will come to see everything that occurs and every person you meet just as important as the other. Equality cannot help but exist in all things as a result. There is not one experience in creation more important than the next.

A lot of people have a lack of value in themselves due to past experiences and conditionings. Some people feel others are better or less than they are. These judgements are there only because of personal beliefs, emotional scarring or society's perceptions of how things 'should be'.

You have incarnated into this realm with the intention of gathering experience. You have been allocated the task of gathering a certain amount and type of experiences. This was actually done by a higher aspect of your soul that exists in the spirit world.

It is a little like going shopping. You write a list of what you need at the shops and as you pick them off the shelf you tick them off your list. Once you have all the items on your list you go home. Sometimes you are not able to pick everything up on your list for some reason, so the missing items go on your next list for the next time you go shopping.

Just like you, your soul has a shopping list of experiences to collect. If all are not gathered before you go home (back into the spirit world) in this incarnation you will add them to your next incarnation.

This is the same for everyone. Almost every earth-incarnating soul is doing the exact same thing. You are gathering your lot (filling your soul's shopping list), everyone else is gathering his or her lot (filling their soul's shopping list), and that's it — there is no wrong experience, only shopping.

The exceptions to the rule are Master Starseed Souls who have put their soul development (spiritual shopping) on hold to help the masses move through their shopping experience, eventually assisting them to ascend into higher consciousness.

A key point to remember: you cannot get your life wrong.

You cannot put anything into your incarnation shopping trolley that is not right for you. Why? Because you have a shopping list with everything on it that you have come for — it is not random. Also, your incarnation/s and all other souls' incarnations are unfolding within a bigger, divine plan.

As a result, you (in fact no-one) can ever get life wrong as Divine Plan is always unfolding in a perfect way with perfect timing. There are no mistakes in Divine Plan simply because God, who created it, cannot make mistakes; it is not in God's makeup.

A lot of people wonder what it is that they should be doing with their lives. Most of us are on this continual search for ways to improve our lot and to make things better.

Whichever perception we choose to have in our lives is really irrelevant in the bigger scheme of things, as all is perfect.

You can never have a wrong experience — it can only be perceived that way, and the result of this negative perception is burden. All experience brings to you what you have come here for, so you can never make a wrong decision. Isn't it great to realise everything you encounter is perfect and in accordance with Divine Plan?

It's only the mind's negative programming that perceives it as otherwise. In any moment, you can choose to see the truth of this and experience joyfulness, or choose to not recognise your divine journey and feel burdened by your life that you perceive to be going the wrong way.

Our minds are often the main culprit when it comes to distorting the truth of our unfoldment. It is the mind that always likes to beat us up over our perceived misgivings. However, all negatives are simply not true in the bigger picture. All negatives are just distorted truths appearing as real, which happens because of our belief in them.

When we give energy to a wrong view we create its existence in our lives. Just because something appears real does not make it so. We can, in any moment, dispel this non-truth simply by perceiving truth. I will explain more about this further on in the book.

I have come across many people who continually struggle to get somewhere. They never realise that they are always exactly where they should be. They try so hard to change their experiences to more positive ones. But often it is this constant striving to get somewhere that gives them the continual experience of discontentment. All the energy that is given to pushing away and resisting what is perceived wrong actually creates more of what is not wanted.

When we struggle to get somewhere we perceive that we are not where we should be. We have a delusionary concept of being in the wrong place or having the wrong experience. But this is a distorted view — non-truth appearing as truth. You cannot get your life wrong.

What is it that makes us think we have to be somewhere else other than where we are right now? Remember, all experience serves the same purpose and has the same value.

So, it does not really matter in the bigger picture what experiences we have. The important thing to remember is this: if you want to have a positive life, then perceive all your current experiences as productive in the bigger picture. Remember, you are doing your spiritual shopping, gathering allocated experiences. When this truth can be seen negatives then become positive and productive.

It is so important to stop and smell the roses wherever you are in life. And there is no better place than where you are right now.

Right now, you are serving your divine purpose. What more would you want to be doing?

Right now you are experiencing divine perfection unfolding. If your experience of this is negative or burdening this tells me you are not seeing energetic truth in this moment.

If you change your negative perceptions to positive, taking the 'bigger picture' view, then joy and happiness appears. Your negative experiences become positive. When you stop attaching to outcomes and expectancies you free your experiences up to allow the joy of the divine to come into your life.

Practice

Sit and ponder the statements below:

- All experience has the same value regardless of how they are perceived. From a higher, more spiritual viewpoint, all experience serves a positive purpose in allowing creation to expand and become enriched.

- I am just an angelic being, existing in a human suit, doing my spiritual experience shopping.

- Equality exists in all life.

- There is no need to make judgement about anyone or any experience, as all experiences I have are what I am here for and are serving a greater, positive purpose.

- I am not less than nor better than anyone else; this is just a judgment coming from my not seeing my higher purpose.

- We are all here as little fragments of God, doing the exactly same thing — experience gathering. As all experiences available in this reality serve the same purpose, there is no distinction or judgment made for better/worse, more valuable/less valuable.

- It does not matter what other people are doing; it has the same value and is for the same higher purpose of exactly what I am doing.

- When I see the truth of my purpose life naturally becomes joyful.

- When the truth is seen allowance occurs, freeing my life to bring the energies of Love and Grace into my day-to-day life.

- I am serious about having a fulfilled life, so I love and value all aspects of myself. Considering everything in existence is *me*, I love and value all life, as all life is me.

Sit now and deeply ponder…

Truth versus Non-Truth

All life functions either in alignment to Divine Plan (Truth) or resistance to it (non-truth). You can never live outside of Divine Plan, but you can experience it from the perception of non-truth, which gives you the experience of negativity.

In a nutshell: Truth is Love and Non-Truth is Fear.

Truth emanates from the Divine (God) and its plan unfolding through consciousness, whereas fear is generated through man-made conditioning and beliefs. Non-truth is actually just a distorted view of truth appearing real.

How much you trust, believe and align to Divine Plan/Truth will determine the quality of your life.

Joy and love, or negativity and struggle ... it's all about your perception.

When you trust in the truth of Divine Plan and trust that your life is unfolding within it perfectly you go a long way towards releasing worry, fear, stress, tension, lack and loneliness.

Divine Plan is always perfect and positive; it knows no other way to be, as it emanates from the love of God. When you have faith and trust in it you have a more direct experience of its quality. Because Divine Plan is based on true, unconditional love, love turns up more in your day-to-day life.

If one is in full alignment to spiritual truth one could not help but have a positive and happy life. It is our resistance to opening up and allowing ourselves to experience Truth and our divine nature that causes negativity. We often resist Truth because it goes against our emotional imprinting and conditioning.

To let go and trust something opposite to what our minds tell us to be true can be very scary. Most people's minds are moulded on fear (non-truth), so to align to Truth means to let go of what we know to be *us*, the basis of our very existence. Our whole foundation of life (according to our mind's beliefs) is challenged. This can be very confronting.

However, Truth is not something you need to struggle or strive to experience. It just requires you to take that first step and let go of your non-truthful beliefs and conditionings. Recognising what is real and what is not is the key. *Key Five* will help with this.

When you do recognise Truth a miracle will appear before your eyes. Positive change on a level that is not conceivable by most people unfolds. Ease, love, abundance and all things you desire turn up in your life without effort — it's magical.

Key One in this book is all about commitment. Letting go of non-truthful beliefs and perceptions is part of that commitment. Retraining yourself to not automatically fall into old non-truthful patterns and energies requires you to be alert to what you are thinking, saying and doing; to recognise quickly what you are giving energy to, and if it is non-truth to do your best to perceive Truth.

Learning to trust your life and its experiences and letting go and allowing will move your life into a new world full of joy and happiness

When you stop trying to push away and resist negativity it loses the very foundation it exists on. Negativity/non-truth is man-made and not a part of true reality. If you do not feed it, it withers and dies.

Negativity appears in life solely because of believing, attaching, resisting or giving energy to something that does not really exist — a non-truthful, delusionary perception of what is really presenting. Negativity/non-truth also appears due to the lack of self-love, which originates from past emotional trauma. We believe we are not good enough, not deserving of love and happiness, and we therefore keep validating this lack of worth through our experiences.

All negative experience you have ever had has occurred because you have believed or aligned to non-truth and have made the 'unreal' appear as 'real'.

I am not saying negative experience does not exist; it does. Why? Because of the powerful ability we as humans have that enables us to create and bring forth into reality whatever we give enough energy to.

Most of what comes to us is what we give attention to.

"Where your attention lies is the point of creation." Where is your attention Right Now!

If you aren't aware of (don't know) where your attention lies you are not aware of what you are creating. You are creating your life unconsciously (random creation). If you are serious about happiness then this is a dangerous thing to do.

When creating unconsciously you have no idea if you are burdening your life with non-truth. This could mean that you are validating all the (false) un-loving beliefs (myths) you hold about yourself. In any moment of time, you could be making your internal non-truth monster bigger and more real simply by giving more energy to non-truthful imprinting.

When we create unconsciously we often follow the path of less resistance. This means a lot of creation comes from your sub-conscious automatic patterns. Most of these are based on distorted, non-truthful past experiences, which are often created out of reaction to perceived wrong doings.

Creating from clarity and awareness decreases your likelihood of negative non-truthful creation.

Your happiness and well-being is dependent on you being AWARE.

A simple rule of thumb:

If my attention is on Truth/love – I create happiness, joy and love.

If my attention is on non-truth/fear – I create burden, pain and suffering.

You will go a long way towards a better life by looking for the spiritual truth in all experiences you have. At the very least, you will diffuse the creation of more non-truth simply by looking for Truth.

Your emotions are a key indicator of what energy you are in alignment to: feeling up — Truth; feeling down — non-truth. Recognising when you are giving energy to non-truth, and knowing what that does to your life (burdens it), you can take responsibility. In that moment of recognition, you can decide to love yourself by diverting your energy generation to truthful creation. Repeatedly doing this helps to hold you in the frequency of Truth. This starts a truthful cycle, and repetition will alter brain patterns to automatically align you to Truth.

There are two main creative cycles our lives can unfold within. One cycle is circular in function; the other is an upward line. The circle mainly consists of non-truth; the upward line is when we are in full alignment to Truth/Divine Plan.

Most people live within the circle. Life is spent attempting to get somewhere, but all a circle does is to allow you to move around within it — it is restrictive. You don't actually get anywhere, as opposed to a line which takes you somewhere.

A circular life gives you moments of joy and love when you are in the upper part of the circle. And at other times you fall into the abyss of negativity and frustration — the downward or bottom part of the circle. During most of our time spent within the circle, we exist somewhere between the extreme top and the bottom. We never actually get a chance to experience real joy and a quality of life, as life is always limited to some degree within the circle. There is always something better to attain or acquire; but, satisfaction is very hard to attain and maintain. Life in a circle is destined to be full of ups and downs. As soon as you feel up, it is only a matter of time before you fall from a great height.

Aligning to non-truth dooms a person to a cyclical high/low circular life. Aligning to Truth brings a person into divine consciousness flow (an upward line). As a result, all experiences become better than the one before. Living on the truthful line is very freeing and joyful. A real, higher quality of life can be experienced without effort or struggle.

Do your best to always perceive and function from spiritual Truth; your happiness really depends on it.

Practice

Sit and reflect on the statement below for a while to get a sense of its truth.

"All positive experience is a direct result of aligning to Truth."

A couple of key points to remember:

- Every time you have a negative feeling or emotion, recognise you must be aligned to non-truth.

- Just recognising when you are aligned to non-truth brings you into alignment to Truth in that moment. It's that simple!

Recognising Where You are in Each Moment

To experience the best possible incarnation you can requires total and continual alignment to Truth. To align in this way requires that you do your best to not function automatically from your old non-truthful imprints, beliefs and perceptions; to be vigilant about when your old patterns arise and activate; and in recognising Truth to change your alignment and outplay of them.

Recognising where you are in each moment

Put simply, if you feel negative it is non-truth. If you feel agitated, angry, sad, critical, judgemental, or any other emotion that is irritating, dark or negative then right at that moment you are in alignment with non-truth. When you align to non-truth you are increasing the likelihood of negative burden in your life.

Why? Well, the reason is simply because all of these emotional states carry the energetic qualities of non-truth. The more you align to non-truth, the more you give it strength in your life and make it appear more real.

When you are in alignment with spiritual Truth, you feel uplifted. This happens because alignment pulls you into the flow of consciousness that carries the qualities of Divine Love. Whenever you are in this flow, you feel nourished, supported, secure, valuable and loved.

Recognising what is not working in your life

Recognising what is not working in your life leads you to recognise non-truthful imprinting. When you are in alignment to Truth things always go right for you and in a positive way.

When you feel things are not working, it means there are reactive energies that are in alignment to non-truth at play, and they are presenting as Truth.

So, what's happening?

Here are some possibilities:

- You currently perceive from the level of non-truth and it is appearing as real, and it is quite possible you are reacting instead of responding.

- You are aligning to the belief in non-perfection and that God's plan is flawed, and you are trying to fix it.

- You are allowing your old imprinted perceptions and beliefs to create non-truthful reactive energy.

- You believe, and have made real, a judgement about yourself that has been imposed upon you by either yourself or another person.

- You are having an experience that you perceive as a personal attack on your value and as a result you react.

A big help in defusing non-truth and its impact on you is simply to recognise the truth of what is happening.

The recognition that you are currently aligning to or giving energy to non-truth is in itself a Truth.

Acknowledging Truth weakens the impact of non-truth.

Being committed to recognising Truth in each presenting experience merges you more and more with Truth. As a result, non-truth appears less and less in your reality. By constantly creating truthful energy through recognition you alter your internal vibration.

Changing your internal vibration into a more truthful frequency is LIFE CHANGING!

A little on the Universal Law of Attraction:

- The universe (God) loves you and always (in every instant) gives you what you ask for.

- Whatever energy resides within is your method of communicating to consciousness.

- Your experience in the external world is simply a validation of what you are experiencing in your inner world.

- Your life (what you see and experience in your day-to-day reality) is always a validation of your internal energetic quality — you see and experience what you are within.

- Your internal energy is in a continual state of vibrational change.

- It can only change to either more non-truth (negative fear-based energy) or more Truth (love-based energy). Whichever way it changes, it will always be validated in external experience.

You are constantly creating energy inside yourself, mostly through what you think and feel and your actions. This energy is continually communicating with the universe (God). Your internal energy is your language and how you speak and communicate to the universe. Universe/God continually gives you exactly what you are asking for through your energy creation. It does this without judgement because it loves you. "Ask and you shall receive."

Very important: What are you currently saying to the universe?

It is important that you remain conscious and aware of what energies you are creating within. A great way to develop quicker recognition speed is through the wonderful practice of *Single Minded Meditation*.

Practice

Single Minded Meditation

This meditation is both a relaxation/inner peace practice and a tool to develop specific skills. It:

- **Increases recognition speed:** Increases the ability to recognise more quickly where your attention lies — on Truth or non-truth. If you recognise you are giving energy to non-truth, you can make change to defuse the negative creation of non-truth.

- **Develops detached observation:** Enables you to observe experience without giving it energy. This is very beneficial when you recognise you are in a position of non-truth. At no time do you want to give energy to non-truth as this will only lead to burden.

- **Improves the quality of your focus:** Better focus means better outcomes in all areas of your life. By improving your focus, you improve the power of creating what you want in life — more Truth.

Single Minded Meditation Practice: Find yourself a comfortable spot to sit. You can sit in a chair or cross-legged on the floor in a meditation position, keeping your back straight. Begin by bringing your focus onto your breath. Breathe in and out through your nose. Observe your breath going in and going out.

Keep your focus on the entrance of your nostrils. Feel the air passing through the entrance of your nostrils as you breathe in, and out of the entrance of your nostrils as you breathe out. Every time you are aware of your mind wandering off onto some other thought, recognise the distraction without judgment, and gently bring your focus back to your nostrils.

Key point:

Every time you align to Truth, you step towards what you seek in your life and you step away from what you don't want.

Stay alert to where your energy lies. Observe your emotional state, which is a key indicator of what you are currently creating.

Acknowledging Truth Dissolves Non-Truth

When you recognise non-truth in your life, it is a time to be joyful. In that moment you receive the gift of an opportunity to make a conscious decision to bring about positive change in your life. You have a choice to seek the Truth in the presenting experience, thereby improving your life.

Without seeing and acknowledging non-truth, you do not get this opportunity. In a funny little way, negative non-truthful experiences are positive. From seeing non-truth, you are faced with a choice or decision to remain either in non-truth and burden your life or to love yourself by making truthful positive change.

Just recognising when you are aligned to non-truth brings you into alignment to Truth.

That is how simple it is to release the negative impact of non-truth. I always do my best to be active in every moment to perceive the Truth in what is presenting. By doing this, I stop the creation of non-truth and create truthfully. Anytime I am in alignment to Truth I empower my life with love.

When Divine Truth is seen, you start to bring into your life the qualities of the Divine. Your internal vibration shifts to a more positive frequency by recognising Truth. No effort is required for this to occur; it simply happens. It is not some secret, complicated process, unachievable or available only to a select few. Removing burden from your life is child's play. In fact, it is so simple most people miss it or just don't get it.

When you see Truth, it is very hard for non-truth to exist. It no longer has a foundation to exist.

To give you an example, if I showed you a glass of water and told you it was an elephant, you would not believe me. It would not matter if I spent the rest of my life telling you it was an elephant, you would never believe me. This non-truthful information has no impact on you. Why? Because you would know this is simply not true; of course it is not an elephant. You know the truth, therefore non-truth cannot impact you, or even be considered.

This is the same for a non-truthful negative energy or experience. Once you see the higher, more spiritual Truth of your experience, negative burdening energy has no foundation to continue to exist. It simply dissolves. WOW!

It is easy to recognise non-truth simply by its nature. Your emotions give you a very clear picture of what you are creating/perceiving. If you feel uplifted you are seeing Truth. If you are feeling negative you believe in non-truth.

In daily activity, when you recognise that you are aligning to non-truth, re-focus on anything that is aligned to Truth. This defuses the generation of non-truthful energy — in a sense you starve your non-truthful monster.

Don't beat yourself up when you recognise that you are aligned to non-truth. By doing so, you support the lack of love you hold towards yourself or perceive within yourself. This self-judgement is just more negative energy abuse and is not a loving thing to do to yourself. It only serves to align you more to non-truth, taking you further from what you seek — happiness.

Practice

Observe your emotions to determine what energy you are feeding and creating. If you become aware you are creating non-truth recognise the truth of what you are doing: *"Right now, I am experiencing a negative emotion or experience. This tells me I am currently giving energy to, or aligning to, a non-truth."* I am making real something that is divinely untrue. This is the only way I can experience a negative.

This truthful recognition and inner statement helps pull you into alignment to Truth. In so doing, it turns me in the direction I want to go, towards happiness. I can also support this with acknowledging that my life is always unfolding perfectly and in accordance to Divine Plan. I cannot get my life wrong; I can only perceive it as such. Just because I perceive something to be wrong does not make it so.

Most non-truth comes from my past conditioning and my belief in what happened at the time. I took on a belief about whom and what I am and made it real. If it is negative it is a non-truthful belief I hold. Just because I have these non-truthful beliefs and conditionings does not mean I have to continue to believe and function from them. In every moment I can choose to see, or at the very least search for, the Truth in the experience. This alone will have a positive impact on my old negative imprinting. It defuses the generation of more non-truth, thereby breaking the restrictive chains and burdening energy non-truthful vibration contains.

The Truth about Reaction

Why do we tend to react to others?

What makes us become reactive?

First off, here I need to re-visit the Universal Law of Attraction. Understanding how this works is a key to understanding why you have the experiences that you have.

Key Point about the Law of Attraction

All experiences you have are a direct result of your internal vibration; you are creating your life through what you vibrate. There are no exceptions to this rule. You are driving the bus of your life and reality.

Contrary to popular belief, no one does anything to you; they are always just the conduits that the universe uses to validate your internal vibration. In a sense, it has absolutely nothing at all to do with the person presenting to you the experiences. In terms of vibration, they are really just showing you … *yourself*.

I have a saying I often use: **"Don't shoot the messenger."**

The big mistake that is often made is we do not see the real reason why we are reactive. We believe the person we are interacting with is the culprit; we externalise blame or judgment. It is very easy to blame someone else for the disharmony we see. However, to see Truth we must recognise what we experience is always what we vibrate within ourselves.

The experiences we have are always a validation from the universe of what is vibrating inside us. Because we do not wish to acknowledge it is really our own energy, we react outwardly to the person: *"How dare you make me see something I buried and don't want to see?"*

Reaction always results from perceiving someone as either judging or attacking us. Reaction often occurs because the person stirs up some emotion or imprint we buried years ago that we hoped we would never see again — out of sight, out of mind.

Important note:

All people are just the delivery vans the universe uses to bring to us a clear picture of what we are within. The person has done you a massive favour by coming into your life and bringing you clarity as to what you hold within.

When we have a negative reaction, we are given in that moment an opportunity to recognise we are holding onto some negativity that is currently burdening our life. All people give us clarity about what we are creating in our lives. They let us know if we are burdening our life with non-truth or supporting our lives with loving Truth.

When we understand why we react we empower our lives. Through seeing Truth, we can better our experiences and learn to respond to life, as opposed to react to life. Response always comes from Truth. We can remain alert to any old reactive patterns popping up, and when we do recognise them we can respond by seeing them as wonderful opportunities to love and value ourselves more.

Response is always the positive approach to situations. Response steps us towards the life we seek. Reaction on the other hand only serves to burden our lives. Sometimes we are not even aware we are reacting until it's too late. Once the fire has been lit it becomes harder to positively respond.

Here's something to think about:

If a delivery van pulled up in your driveway and the driver came to your door and handed you a parcel would you get angry with him/her?

Obviously, you wouldn't. Why would you get angry or reactive to someone giving you a parcel or present? That would just be plain silly.

Well, every day of your life you have delivery vans pulling up in your reality in the form of people and experiences. They are all giving you what you have ordered from the universe — a gift of Truth. Your order comes in the form of what they do and say, and then you react or respond to them depending on your conditioning, patterns and beliefs.

Your internal vibration is what is being validated from people and experiences. They are just the means/transport to bring an external version of yourself to be validated. And if it is negative energy it gives you an opportunity to love and value yourself more by positively responding to what you see before you.

We should be thanking all the people that annoy us. They are truly gifts in our lives, presenting to us great opportunities to love and value ourselves even more. It is amazing how all souls support each other to move towards Truth in this way.

I strongly recommend you get yourself a copy of my audio recording about the cause of anger. This recording will help you enormously to understand why we have the experiences we have. Simply by listening to this, you will totally change the way you think and feel towards all people.

This recording is one of a series titled *Essential Teachings*. This particular recording is titled *The Cause of Anger*.

Practice

Many people hold onto resentment and issues toward people that they perceived did them wrong. This burdens their life as they are feeding non-truth in their bodies, making it stronger. These energies of non-truth are disruptive to harmony.

It also changes their internal vibration, bringing to them more people and situations that will validate what they currently vibrate within — negativity.

Burdening energy within brings more burdening energy externally through experience.

Therefore, if you are currently holding onto issues, it is in your interest to release their non-truthful energies, especially if you are serious about having a joyful, loving and easy life.

So, how can you do this?

There is a wonderful Buddhist practice called *Tonglen Meditation* that is a simple yet powerful way to dissolve issues towards someone.

Tonglen Meditation Practice

Start off with single-minded meditation to bring your focus onto singular attention. Then visualise the person that you feel anger or resentment towards. On your in-breath imagine and feel that you are taking from them all that hurts and burdens them, drawing this then into your own heart centre.

Important point:

As the energy of all this enters your heart centre, imagine and feel all of it dissolving into pure love. You are not taking this energy on; you are instantly dissolving it into love in your heart space.

Now, on your out-breath feel pure love flowing back to this person, nurturing and nourishing their life. Your intention for doing this is a pure intent to help that person's life.

Keep repeating this breathing sequence for at least ten to twenty minutes. By regular practice of this you will let go of all of the negative feelings and thoughts you have towards this person.

This will not only benefit your life, but theirs as well.

Creating Energy Flow

Probably the most important ingredient in creating a happy and contented life, full of ease and love, is energy flow. When energy is allowed to move freely in and through the human energy field and internal energy system, hardship and burden naturally disperses.

One of the first areas to look at to create energy movement is *communication*. Most people never fully say what's on their minds. They hold onto thoughts and feelings to keep the peace, or out of fear of being judged as not good enough or second rate. When we don't communicate what we feel we stagnate our internal energy system, which starts to have a negative impact on our life as a result. Uncommunicated thoughts and feelings don't magically dissolve and go away. They stay within, causing all sorts of havoc and disharmony.

Never hold onto anything. Communicating what you think and feel is one of the ways to value and love yourself more. It is out of love that we achieve sustained happiness, which is what every person on Earth is seeking. It is those little thoughts and feelings that we don't get off our chest that do the most negative, stagnating damage.

Never be concerned what people think about you and what you communicate.

The old saying, *"What someone thinks of you is none of your business,"* is important to remember.

No person alive should have a problem with you honestly saying what's on your mind. If they do then it's their issue, not yours.

Don't beat yourself up over someone else's issues by being self-critical or judgmental. Don't suppress your feelings and emotions for the sake of not rocking the boat. This is a very unloving thing to do to yourself, and you deserve much better than that.

If you do not communicate everything that's on your mind, you are making a decision to energetically abuse yourself. You are validating that you don't deserve happiness and a good life. The truth is you deserve an absolutely amazing life. You have entered into this incarnation as a very special soul, doing a very special job (gathering three-dimensional experiences); this should be valued and honoured.

Part of your commitment to attaining a fulfilled life, and also to honour your soul's journey, is to always do your best to love yourself in every moment. Communication is one of the ways to effectively do that. Of course, there are two ways to communicate: gently with love or and negative aggression with reaction.

Take a big, deep breath and say what's on your mind right now, in a loving way, without judgment; just express how you feel and that's it. All communication should be done without judgment or blame — remember no one has ever done anything against you. You have created all experiences, including the perceived bad ones, to give you opportunities to see some energy within you that is unloving. As you already know from earlier Keys, all experiences serve a positive, equal purpose in making you more whole. No communication should carry any form of attack, blame or judgment. That is a very unloving, non-truthful way to communicate.

Communication creates internal energy movement. Movement washes away what is not real (fear-based non-truth)

The three other common causes for energy flow stagnation are what I call *The Three Poisons*. They are: **Attachment, Resistance and Control.**

The first poison: *Attachment*

Attachment, as the name suggests, holds onto things. Most people attach to people and things because of insecurity, which is a lack of self-love. We fear loss and as a result hold on tight to everything that makes us feel whole, supported and complete. Holding on, or attaching, gives us a false sense of security.

Attachment hinders natural consciousness flow — everything you seek in life comes from consciousness

In the case of internal energy flow, attachment does to your energy channels what fat does to your arteries. The more you attach to things, the more burdened your energies become. This makes everything a little more sluggish and negative. Attaching to positive good things is just as bad as attaching to negatives; they both clog up the system.

One of the most common forms of attachment is attachment to our partners. Many of us do this because of our misguided love for our partners. However, the act of attaching to a partner is really a very unloving thing to do. All this will serve is to create a breeding ground for resentment. When we attach to our partner, we hinder the natural unfolding of their life. On a deep sub-conscious level this is recognised by them; eventually, you will be resented for doing this.

It is only a matter of time before this happens in any relationship. When it does, arguments will occur or someone will suppress their feelings and burden their life, eventually manifesting illness as a result. If you truly love your partner you should do your best to not hinder them on any level. When their life is allowed to unfold unrestricted, they will love you more. When you detach and fully communicate with your partner, you are creating the best possible energy flow for your relationship to succeed and this will ultimately create unity.

Whatever you hold onto — people, places, possessions, anything at all — you are only making your life more negative and more difficult as a result. If you truly loved yourself you would not do this. When you grasp and hold on, you push away everything the universe wishes to give you — joy, abundance, love, ease and allowance. Everything you seek comes from universal consciousness flow, but more on this later.

Some people hold onto things out of a false sense of security. True security comes from self-love, not material possessions or people.

Security is an internal thing and is never reliant on external objects or people.

Once you look outside of yourself for happiness, love and contentment you miss the point.

Let go of what you are currently attaching to — your life will love you for it. If you cannot bring yourself to let go you really need to look at why you cannot. On some level you fear lack or are feeling vulnerable; these are energies of non-truth.

Let's now look at the second poison, the energy of *resistance*.

A key point about resistance: What you resist persists

If you are trying to push something away — something you perceive you do not want — you are in fact giving energy to it. Because of your focus on the issue, you have manifested vibrational change within. As a result, the Universal Law of Attraction will manifest the thing or situation in your external reality as a validation of what you just created. You inadvertently create the very thing you don't want: a very important process to remember.

Another key point here is: Where your attention lies is the point of creation. Your happiness is dependent on your being aware of what you are creating.

By focussing on something you are trying to get rid of, you give it lots of energy and empower it. This will in effect only make it harder to shift. Believe it or not, but one of the best ways to shift anything at all in life is to *allow it to be there*. When you allow, you don't restrict energy movement. If the experience you are trying to get rid of is negative it will quickly dissolve into a positive Truth. Why? Because movement is a quality of divine consciousness, and consciousness is a vibration of Truth. All Divine Truth is positive, loving and supportive. Consciousness will actually flush the negative non-truth away.

Looking at it another way, why would you ever want to push anything away from your life? Remember, all experiences you have serve your purpose as a human. You are just a soul existing in a human suit to gather energetic experiences; all experiences have a positive, divine purpose. If the experience appears as negative it is that way because you made it negative, through a false view of Truth.

The last of the energetic poisons to look at is *Control*.

Control, just like attachment and resistance, creates restriction in energy flow. Restriction of flow only causes more burden and hardship. Our endocrine glands are put under enormous amounts of stress when we restrict flow. To maintain homeostasis (optimal functionality) our endocrine glands rely on receiving energetic nourishment from our chakras. This can only be achieved if the energy channels that supply this nourishment are open and free flowing. When we control our lives we hinder the free flow of energy to the glands. This starves them of nourishment and eventually the glands are not able to produce the right amount of hormones at the right time. This ultimately leads to illness on some level.

We often control because we do not believe our lives are unfolding accurately. We perceive our life as not being the way it should be. As a result, we try to control its unfoldment to make sure we get it right. We do this because we do not understand the truth about the perfection of Divine Plan and its unfoldment. We control because we are either fearing getting our life wrong or we are holding onto something that we feel makes us complete.

Everything in existence is unfolding in accordance to Divine Plan. Divine Plan is the outward flow of God's conscious intention to create and be enriched. I will let you into a little secret — *God's plan has no mistakes.* God could not make a mistake in anything it does, even if it tried. The energy of 'wrong', or 'failure', is not in its makeup. Remember, *you can only ever create what you are.* God is the pure essence of true unconditional love and can only create or experience from this vibration.

It is absolutely impossible to get your life wrong. It can only ever appear as though it is because we keep trying to fix it.

Stop fixing and allow!

We have a belief, due to past non-truthful conditioning, in imperfection. Because of this distorted belief we spend our lives trying to make perfect something that is already perfect.

Perfection is perfect; it does not need fixing or changing. It just needs to be experienced for what it is — perfection.

If we actually got out of our own way and detached and allowed our lives would naturally be joyful. All stress and worry would disappear. Why? Because we, and all of our experiences, are a part of a Divine Plan that holds no negatives. Negative experience is a result of non-truthful beliefs and conditionings.

A short word on spiritual consciousness

Universal consciousness is the spiritual energetic flow that brings to you everything you seek and desire. Universal consciousness can also be seen as a continual outpouring of God's intention. It is vital to allow this energetic flow to move in and through your life unhindered.

You can look at spiritual consciousness as water flowing down a river. Attachments, resistance, control and repressed emotional issues create dams. When this occurs, spiritual consciousness and all of its qualities and gifts cannot flow to you and the result can be unhappiness and ill-health.

The natural state of divine consciousness is one of continual movement. To be in alignment with it requires that you stay in a state of non-restrictive allowance. Repressing issues and energies stops this from occurring and that is why it is so important to openly and joyfully embrace all experiences. Embrace them, but allow them to move in and through you without attachment, control or resistance.

Most past conditioning is not in alignment with allowing the free movement of Divine Truth and as a result imprints and clogs natural energy flow in the body. To be in flow you have to allow all non-truthful and truthful energies to disperse and move through. Once again, you cannot resist, attach or control.

Because the majority of your life is based and structured on non-truth, this is not always easy. In fact, most of what your life is based on has to change. However, a positive spiritual life is all about energy movement. The more you create, the more you come into alignment with Truth and consciousness.

Any opportunity to create energy movement should be embraced, regardless of whether it makes you feel uncomfortable. Remember, God and/or Consciousness is always in a constant unhindered state of movement/allowance.

Movement mimics consciousness

Loving unconditionally mimics consciousness.

Aligning to truth mimics consciousness.

Mimicking consciousness allows you to experience more of consciousness.

Living with detachment and allowance is a spiritually conscious thing to do.

With detached allowance your internal energy naturally floods with more consciousness. Due to the Universal Law of Attraction, more of the qualities of consciousness (love) will show up in your external reality and experiences.

When you do more of what consciousness does, you experience more of what consciousness is.

An interesting point about consciousness flow:

Universal consciousness is a continual upward flow. When you are in full alignment to it every experience you have is always better than the one before it.

Practice

Recognition and Allowing Practice

This is a great practice to clear non-truthful negative imprinting that is currently burdening your life.

1. *Bring to your mind a past negative experience.*

2. *Sense where you feel this in your body (as all unresolved past negative experiences imprint somewhere in the body).*

3. *Now put your full focus onto the feeling in the body and not the experience itself.*

4. *Don't try to resist this energy you are now aware of, and do your best to fully open and allow it to be there. Know that whatever you are currently experiencing in life (including negative imprinting) is there and is a part of divine perfection. Every experience you ever have is the right one for you; you cannot have a wrong experience in your life.*

5. *Be happy now that you are having a more direct experience of your perfection unfolding. (Why would you ever want to change your life and its experiences from unfolding in the perfect way and perfect time in accordance with Divine Plan)*

Allow any discomfort you may feel during the process described above to be there, as this is just the recognition of a non-truth and it is okay for it to be there. It's okay to feel whatever you feel.

When you allow this negative imprint to be in your body it naturally starts to move toward having a positive frequency and nature. Remember, negative non-truthful energies only exist as a result of resistance, control or attachment. So, all negative energies will lessen or fully dissolve when they are not fed energy. When you allow their existence but detach from them you starve them of food and eventually they die.

To start the process of lessening the impact of negative energy in your life is that simple.

Creating energy flow – key points to remember

Full communication, with the expressing of all thoughts and feelings, is vital to create positive experiences and ultimate contentment within all interactions with people.

When you attach regularly to non-truth, you will eventually have negative experiences popping up on a mental, emotional, physical or spiritual level. It's unavoidable. When you allow the energy of these experiences to exist and don't hinder their natural flow they dissolve.

Happiness and a fulfilled life are all about energy flow. Where there is flow, joy resides; where there is stagnation, there is always burden.

To learn more in depth about the three common causes of restricted energy flow, grab a copy of my Essential Teachings audio titled *The 3 Poisons*.

Remember: All experiences you have are the right ones in the right moment of time.

If an experience is negative, the quickest way to move through it is to not give it any energy by having an attachment to it. When you acknowledge its presence without attaching to it (detached observation), you allow movement. Movement is a quality of consciousness flow, which is always positive. Movement always brings positive experience.

The only reason why we get ill is because we do not allow energy movement. When we hold onto issues and emotions or have attachment to people and/or situations we create stagnation.

What to do when old non-truthful imprints or beliefs arise

Recognise the truth of what is being presented and be very happy you actually recognised it. Celebrate! Acknowledge the truth about it and allow its presence in your life. Re-affirm truth and allow, knowing that all is perfect and in divine order.

Non-Separation

What You See is You

When I talk about non-separation, I am referring to the energy of all life. Science tells us everything is energy and that all energy is a part of a greater whole. In a nutshell, you are a part of all things manifested in this life and all other levels of existence/reality. I will go out on a limb here and make the statement that, *"Everything is a part of God, so in fact being a piece of this energy actually makes you God"*.

"Hi, God. Pleased to meet you, my name is God, also."

So, how is God treating him or herself today? That's a good question you may want to ask yourself.

Are you beating yourself up by being judgmental or negative to others?

Are you worrying or stressing-out over some non-truth?

When you really understand the concept of non-separation you have to agree that everything is a part of you and you are a part of everything. In a sense, everything you see is you.

Just think about this a second ... "Everything I See is Me". That means every person you meet is another part of you — you are energetically linked. No, it is not only that they are reflecting your stuff back through the Law of Attraction. Yes, this is happening, but the main reason is because they actually are a piece of whom and what you are.

Every person, animal, plant, mineral — everything — is actually another part of you or the greater whole.

A key point to recognise also is this: You impact the whole with everything you do. You either enhance it by creating Truth or you burden it by creating non-truth. So, if you are really serious about being loving towards yourself, you have to likewise be loving towards all Life.

Knowing that everything you see is you, the big question here is how are you going to treat yourself?

The key to what you seek — happiness — comes from loving self. So, to enable yourself to love, you need to consider directing this energy towards everyone you encounter. That means you can no longer be critical and feel anger or resentment towards another, as they are actually you.

So, how can you be more loving to yourself? One of the best ways is through being of service, which I will discuss further on in this book.

My external experiences are the accurate picture of my internal vibration.

Another aspect of "All that I see is me" is the functionality of the Universal Law of Attraction. I have gone over how this works in previous keys, but it doesn't hurt to repeat this important concept.

The Law of Attraction states: What I vibrate within will always be reflected and/or validated in all of my external experiences. In other words, my internal vibration colours all experience. In fact the easiest way to see the state of your internal vibration only requires that you look at what is happening in your life. Are you struggling to achieve happiness? If so, this tells me you have non-truthful disharmony vibrating away inside of you.

Every time I experience disharmony in my external world I get very happy. Why? Because I have an opportunity to love myself a little more by constructively linking into the disharmony I feel and allowing it to be there without struggle (the allowing practice from *Key 8*). This helps to dissolve and wash away the non-truth, thereby bringing me into more

Truth/Love through the flow of consciousness. Every time I experience negativity, I am given the opportunity to love myself more.

My negative experiences now serve as a wonderful tool to become more aligned to Truth and therefore afford myself the option to have a higher quality of happiness in my life.

Negatives become positives.

Practice

Sit now and deeply ponder the concept of non-separation:

* Know that everything is actually a part of who and what you are.

* Everything I see is me.

* Treat others with love and value; by doing so you love and value yourself, as they are you.

* When I experience negativity in my life I am just seeing the negativity within being validated and reflected back to me through another aspect of myself. Be thankful you get to see that negativity because in that moment you have an opportunity to take positive truthful action and love yourself more.

* A good question to ask yourself whenever you feel negative is, "How would God respond?"

* Another great question is, "What's the loving thing to do for myself right now, meaning **all** of me?" (that is, me and everyone else who make up the whole)

Sit and deeply ponder these things, as they are important ingredients for creating a happy and fulfilled life.

True Love

When you are in the full flow of true unconditional love, you are directly experiencing your wholeness. When you are in love's flow you are not reliant on any external experience, thing or person to feel complete or happy — you are self-empowered.

As a result, love and the joy it brings cannot be taken from you. Your love is something within yourself and is not tarnished or determined by what someone else says, thinks or does. When self-love is generated, seen and felt, insecurity and emotional dependency becomes a thing of the past. Any need to seek approval or validation simply dissolves, as you are complete.

True love is internal, not external.

An important thing to realise is: True love comes from within you; it is not external.

If you are reliant on love from another person in order to feel complete and contented, you miss the point of what love is.

You are looking externally for something that is lacking within you — love.

To give you an analogy, let's say your body runs on electricity. You have a powerhouse inside of you to generate all the electricity you need. This allows you to function perfectly, independent of any external source — you are self-supportive and whole. But if your internal power plant broke down and you had to plug into an external power generator, you would be reliant on that external source to keep functioning. You then start to function without wholeness; you become incomplete. This becomes a very insecure existence; at any time you could be disconnected.

If you are relying on someone to make you feel love and/or loved what happens if they leave? What happens to your wholeness? All of a sudden love is gone and emptiness and pain occurs, and you fall apart. When the love you experience is generated from within, it is stable, safe and secure, giving you true wholeness. This gives you an authentic life. If you truly love yourself it does not matter what anyone does; it does not change that love or that Truth.

When love is generated from within, external love can be experienced in a more profound way.

Love is never found outside of yourself. The love, or lack of it, you experience from others is always a reflection and meter of the amount of love you have within yourself. You can only ever have what you are. If you have love within, love shows up in all of your experiences. This also greatly increases the likelihood of attracting a loving partner to your life.

If you love 'you', other people will too.

If you want more love in your life, then look for ways to love 'yourself' more. When you are full of self-love and self-value you become very attractive to other people. People tend to do more loving things for you; your internal love impacts on them in that way.

Real love is all about removing resistance to energy flow.

True love happens when we are living in a full state of detached allowance (unhindered energy movement). When we let all experiences and energy move in and through our lives without restriction, we are being loving to ourselves. This is true love.

The real meaning and understanding of love is all about energy flow; your level of self-love is determined by how much you let go of whatever you are holding onto.

The less resistance you have, the more love you experience.

When you let go of what makes you feel uncomfortable or fear you love yourself in that moment. This includes letting go of emotions, people, momentary dependence, objects and jobs — anything at all you have an attachment to. If it restricts or hinders your natural flow you are not being loving to yourself.

If you restrict your divine self from unfolding in the way God intended you are doing a great disservice to your life.

You are not valuing who you are — a sacred soul doing a sacred job. Whenever you do this you burden or make harder some level of your unfoldment.

If you are not doing your best to be in alignment to, and allow, energetic flow you are not doing your best to love yourself.

If this is the case, the question that needs answering here is: Why not?

Why don't you feel worthy of love?

What is it that is stopping you from full allowance and detachment?

Why do you choose to not be committed to having a loving and happy life? Know that any restriction to your internal energy flow is an unloving thing to do.

Is it because you do not feel worthy or you think you're undeserving of success?

If you do not feel you are worthy or deserving it is because you believe in something from your past that is non-truthful and appearing as real in your life, and you are taking it on as a Truth?

Do you do this because to let go of something unloving would mean you have to let go of something you hold as true and safe in your life? A lot of what we base our lives on is non-truth and is therefore unloving. So, to let go of these things makes us feel very uneasy and often scares us. The irony here is what makes us feel uncomfortable is often what can be an effective catalyst to creating self-love.

Past non-truthful perception of experiences prevents us from generating self-love.

Your fears and perceptions of your value are often the result of past emotional conditioning. Way back when you were younger, you most likely had an experience that you perceived as validating you not being as valuable or as important as other people. Ever since then, because of the emotional imprint you created at the time, you are now continually attracting to you experiences to validate what you vibrate within (lack of value and importance).

It may have been as simple as an experience of your mum wanting to go shopping and being in a hurry. Let's say you are six years old and you want to go shopping with her, but because your mum is running late to go somewhere else later she tells you that you cannot come. She does this to save time, not because she doesn't love you. But as a six year old you perceive that as "I am not good enough to go," or "Mummy does not love me anymore." As a result, you believe something about the experience that isn't true. Of course, your mum loves you; she is just in a hurry.

From this moment on, because of the non-truthful belief you now have about yourself, you keep attracting experiences to re-affirm you are not good enough. This takes you further and further away from love and value.

As a result, you start repressing and restricting energy movement and flow even more, in the hope you will not have more experiences to shine a light on your perceived lack of value. You do not want to ever see again the flaws you 'see' in who and what you are. This just makes you feel less loved and valuable.

As a result of this, you start living a life full of non-truthful self-beliefs, so you continue to avoid at all costs your emotional issues. In a sense, you are creating burden and hardship because you continue to believe a value judgment you made way back then.

Many people continually use past experiences to validate why they feel bad, cannot succeed or are unhappy. In fact they will continually be given new external experiences to support they are not good enough. Past conditioned emotional cruxes are an easy way to validate 'poor me'.

At some stage, however, we all need to take a stand and choose to not burden ourselves; to make a stand and be brave enough to let go of our entire negative past experiences and conditioning that are negatively impacting on us right now.

This means no holding onto emotional issues, feelings of lack, worry, stress, judgment of self and others, anger, being critical of people and situations, no blaming or complaining and so on.

Until we learn to fully express how and what we feel we will never be free from burden and emptiness. Happiness will only be a dream. Love cannot exist in a person that restricts internal energetic movement.

True love is all about energy flow — where there is flow there is love.

Truth is that when you are repressing or restricting flow in any way you are not loving yourself.

What most people perceive love to be, it actually is not.

Many people think they are in love, or being loving. But what most have and create is what I call *conditional love*, which is not love at all. This conditional love that we all create is based on our insecurities and fears, which are non-truth. Love can never have a foundation of non-truth.

True love does not have conditions.

I have thought about love a lot over the years and have come to the conclusion that until we can function in a continual state of detached allowance, we as humans will not be able to experience love in its purest form.

Our past conditioning and the non-truthful perceptions that we all hold about who and what we are prevent us from having a direct experience of true love.

Until we ascend out of our fear-based reality and conditioning we will only experience the man-made version of love. Until we stop looking for love externally, we will not be able to experience the truth of love. Until we can allow the unconditional love emanating from our hearts to rise to the surface to dispel our non-truthful beliefs and perceptions, and then detach from their burden, we will not be able to truly experience what love is.

True unconditional love can only be experienced in others as a reflection of directly experiencing our true innate nature. It has to come from within and then, and only then, can we grasp its real beauty.

Practice

What are some of the ways I can develop more true love?

Some of this development can occur by understanding more of what love is, valuing your place in the big scheme of things and knowing you are an integral part of the whole.

It is being kind, supportive and loving towards yourself in every moment. This also means not creating non-truthful negative energies.

Don't hold onto emotions and issues. Always fully communicate what you think and feel, regardless of what people might say or think. Communication creates energy movement, which is a loving thing to do.

Learn to take time out for *you*. Do something for yourself, not for others. Value your time, especially your 'Quiet Me Time'.

Do your best to emulate what you see as loving and positive within others.

Always be sincere and never consciously create in a negative way.

Never do anything with expectancy. Expectancy is always restrictive and unloving.

The more love you have within, the less fear exists.

In each moment be what you actually are — a beautiful piece of God, enriching all life through experience.

Never involve yourself in negative gossip or spread malicious things, thoughts and judgments.

Always remember where your point of creation (attention) is — is it truthful, supportive and loving or are you being un-loving?

You are never alone in life and creation; you are always a part of a greater whole. All the support you ever need to be more loving to others and yourself exists right in your heart — right now.

I have a saying that I love: *"Everything we seek as humans dwells within our hearts. The Heart is the abode of True Unconditional Love – GO THERE..."*

Always remember, God loves and honours you in every moment.

If you want to experience more love in your life, be more loving to others — what you put out you get back (Law of Cause and Effect).

Don't support others in non-truthful creation. In other words, if someone is complaining about other people don't get involved. Whenever you recognise non-truth do your best to align and give energy to the truth presenting within it.

Practice technique for connecting to a deeper level of love

I have a wonderful meditation practice I channelled from spirit that I would like to share with you. It can have quite a profound impact if done with the right motivation and intention.

> Set a pure intent to directly connect to the heart and love of God within your heart space. This intent needs to be sincere and heartfelt. You need to have a great desire to be at one with God's heart and love.
>
> Once this intent is set, bring your consciousness and focus into the central energy channel (sometimes called Sushumna), which is in the space between the two energy vortexes of the heart chakra (that emanate out from both the front and back of the heart chakra, like two funnels). There is a space between the two, within the heart chakra, that appears like

emptiness. You will have to move your focus back and forth in this space until you feel this energy gap. Once you find it, you should notice a radiant light or a deep sense of stillness, or even a feeling of nothingness, come over you. Once you find it, relax and just 'be' in this space without any effort. Just be open and one with your desire to connect with God's love and heart. Allow yourself to just 'be' within your heart space and intention.

Sit for as long as you like...

There are many ways to support the love within you. The best thing is to always look for the truth in all experiences. Be vigilant in re-aligning to truth when you find yourself in non-truth.

Remember, truth feels uplifting as opposed to non-truth, which feels heavy, negative and burdening. Quietly observe your emotional state to gauge which energy you are creating, and always do your best to create from love/Truth.

Don't judge yourself in any way if you perceive you have done wrong. Remember, your life is always unfolding in the perfect way and time in accordance to Divine Plan. Judgment is the energy of non-truth and is burdening.

Have acceptance for what people do in their lives, don't restrict or control — allow all experience. Remember, they are merely gathering experience, just like you; no judgement is necessary.

Do your best always to create energy movement through the expression of thoughts and feelings — in a loving way. Love and value your divineness; contrary to what you may perceive about yourself, you are a very special soul doing very special things.

You are, and have always been, a divine fragment of God, and you should always see yourself as the most wonderful, whole beautiful soul that you are.

It's all up to you ... Be the love of who you are and bring benefit to all Life. Right now you have this opportunity — embrace it.

Choices

The beautiful thing about being human is we each have the ability to make choices. In any moment of life you can decide to make change and bring new experiences. Your ability to choose will never be taken from you as long as you have a functioning brain. It does not matter where you find yourself in life; if you do not like what you are experiencing, choose to do something different.

This may come in the form of a shift in how you think and feel, or may be a decision to move house, change jobs, leave your partner, dress differently or change friends — anything at all. Every time you make a choice to do something different you instigate internal energy movement, which is a good thing to do.

The worst thing you can do in regards to choices and decision-making is not making one. When you sit on the fence struggling over which way to choose, you stagnate energy flow. This will always bring burden and most often will make it harder to make the decision you are struggling with. The longer you leave a decision the harder it gets.

A good thing to keep in mind about decisions is this: If you do not like the outcome of your choice or decision it is easily fixed — make another one.

When we pull apart human life and really look at the simplicity within how it all works, we see that in any given moment we are actually presented with only two choices. That's it. That's how hard and complicated your life really is — two choices presenting in any given moment.

"What are these two choices?" I hear you asking

1. Choose to perceive negatively (non-truth) and burden my life, or
2. Choose to perceive positively (Truth) and bring ease and joy to my life.

This is the choice that is presented to you in every given moment.

Which decision you make in choosing either one way or the other will shape and colour your life today, next week, next month and so on.

If you are continually experiencing hardship in your day-to-day life you are choosing to create from non-truth that is resonating somewhere within. You are allowing your non-truthful imprinting to dictate your decision-making processes. This is the only way you can have negativity.

So, what happens when I choose to negatively react?

My mind perceives the experience as an attack (as negative). As a result, I create an internal reactive energy that is experienced as a feeling in my body. I have allowed the external experience to validate a non-truthful, non-loving belief I hold about myself. In that moment I have given energy to and empowered my original negative imprint that brought me the experience in the first place.

As a result of this negative energy shift within my body's vibrations, I increase the likelihood of attracting more negative experiences to validate what I now vibrate. This can create a continuing cycle of negative attraction and negative self-empowerment *ad infinitum*.

What positive thing can I do when I experience negative reaction?

Well, first, how can I choose differently?

The negative physiological experience that I create (the direct result of the perceived negative experience or situation) gives me the opportunity to observe that I am aligning to a non-truthful energy imprint within myself. (Non-truthful energy has been validated by the negative experience). The experience literally shines a light on the truth of what is actually happening — that I am currently aligning and/or giving energy to a non-truth. This is the only way to have negative experience.

This recognition alone moves me into alignment to truth (I see the truth of what is really occurring, not what my mind's past conditioning wants me to believe).

I now see this experience as positive and productive rather than negative. I see it as an opportunity to recognise I have a negative burdening energy imprint within. This recognition gives me a wonderful opportunity to love and value myself more. I choose to see positive truth as opposed to burdening non-truth.

This is something to get very happy about. This alone, in most people, creates a positive change within their lives.

It all comes down to *perception*. No one does anything *to* me. I make a choice about how I perceive the experience, depending on my past conditioning and the level of clarity, or the lack there of, in seeing truth.

Here's another way of looking at this:

When someone judges me, gets angry with me or does something to annoy me I recognise they are part of an external experience that I have created through the Universal Law of Attraction (Remember the delivery van analogy from *Key Seven*).

This experience has appeared to validate a previously created internal vibration that is aligning to non-truth. This means the experience is showing me the vibration of that non-truth which is still vibrating within me right now.

This whole experience then can be seen as a gift; so thank those involved or the situation, or indeed God, for it.

What happens next is up to me — I have the ability to choose what I create next, regardless of how I have done it in the past. My sub-conscious automatic patterns may want to push me down the usual way. But if this way is negative I have the ability to choose to make a different decision. I can choose to move towards Truth instead of non-truth and in so doing move me one step closer to what I seek — sustained happiness and love.

In all experiences and situations I have two choices as to how I react or respond:

I can now make an internal decision to either

a) **React** = Act automatically from non-truth
   To do what I've always done → disempower and burden my life

b) **Respond** = Act from Truth/love
   To make a new choice → positively empower my life

Practice

Remember, you always have a choice in how you create your life, even if you think you don't. It all depends on how committed you are to having a happy and loving life. Recognise when you are creating from non-truth, and do your best to consciously decide to create Truth. Being vigilant in this will dramatically change your life and experiences — it's all up to you.

Making decisions brings energy movement. Where there is movement there is love.

Creating movement through decision-making allows more consciousness to flow into your life. Remember, consciousness holds all of the positive things that you seek.

Any resistance to making decisions are there because of non-truthful fear. Merely feeling insecure or having a fear of the unknown outcome of doing something differently should not stop you from making positive change. After all, you deserve a happy and loving life, full of ease and abundance.

When you are faced with negativity and/or fear, do the following:

RECOGNISE that your attention lies on a non-truth and you are feeding it and making it bigger.

OBSERVE without attachment/judgement (detached observation); allow it to be there without struggle.

REALIGN your attention with Truth and watch it dissolve. See the truth of what is happening; this empowers you and starts to dissolve non-truth and fear.

This process is a very effective tool to move your life towards a more loving existence. By doing this you are consciously creating. This will bring you closer to the life you seek — one of happiness and love. You are also retraining your mind's patterning to be more in alignment to Truth.

This is a very good thing.

In functioning in this way, the ease with which you currently create pain, suffering and burden (non-truthful disharmony) will automatically be the same ease with which you create love, joy and sustained happiness (harmony).

You will achieve this simply by making better choices.

An interesting thing about brain patterns

Any truthful recognition and choosing of new, different responses will be a cause for concern for the well-worn neural pathways that exist. The brain will say, "Hey, what's going on here? Something is different!" Different choices and decisions are being made.

This **CONSCIOUSLY** repeated new, truthful decision-making will create new neural pathways. The old neural pathways, through lack of use, will perish and die. The new neural pathways will become stronger and stronger the more they are used.

New positive automatic responses to life's experiences will be created that are in alignment to truth/love. By the Universal Law of Attraction, love, joy and happiness will start to 'show up' more and more in your external reality; your life experiences.

Then it becomes very easy — you will be having more loving and joyful experiences in your life, without effort, and less painful burdened ones until, maybe, you attain 'the end of suffering'.

Making decisions: Key points to remember:

- You can never make a wrong decision; it can only appear that way due to delusionary perception.

- All decisions are in alignment to Divine Plan, regardless of how you perceive the outcome.

- If you are unhappy with a decision simply make another one. A point I should add here is if you feel unhappy about a decision you are in alignment to a non-truth.

- Be joyful about all decisions as they always bring to you perfection in Divine Plan.

- The more decisions you make, the more energy movement you create. This increases the likelihood of bringing more consciousness flow through your life. Consciousness flow holds the loving qualities of God. Bringing more of this into your life will greatly enhance it.

Being Of Service

Being of service is the highest form of spiritual practice for any human being. All highly evolved beings that have walked this planet all had one thing in common — being of service. Jesus, the Buddha and all enlightened beings from all beliefs and walks of life have brought understanding and awakening through their ability and pure intent to be of service to mankind.

As a human you can align to the spiritual consciousness of these great enlightened souls, and all the many others that have come before you, by simply being of service. Being of service is a very good way to help each of us grow and awaken to the ascension process we are all moving through.

The act of being of service is one of the highest aspects of being God in a Human Suit.

When you are being of service to other aspects of yourself (people and all life), without condition, you are creating life in natural alignment with the energy of the bigger piece of God.

Why? Because this is the energy God radiates.

God's whole purpose for existence is to emanate the pure loving energy of true unconditional love, to bring benefit to all aspects of itself. This includes all human life, as we are all fragments of the whole. This is the highest form of being of service. This giving of love unconditionally is the spiritually highest energy in existence.

If you are undecided as to what you should be doing in this life, or are looking for your true purpose, well, the highest purpose you can serve is to be of service. Being unconditionally of service is the most loving thing you can do for yourself and others.

Practice

So, how can you be of service?

There are many ways you can be of service. It can be as little as giving a hand to someone in need who you meet out and about in your day — a friend or stranger who you see is struggling with their lives.

Maybe it is just to be available for company for someone who is lonely.

You may show loving kindness, tolerance and consideration for others that you come in contact with.

You may offer words of truth so people can see alternatives to their current perceptions. A key point, however, is to never impose upon others your beliefs without them asking for your opinion.

There are so many ways to be of service; it just requires a little thought on your behalf. Whenever you create truthful energy or vibration you are being of service to the whole. You are supporting all life with love and grace.

When you do things that support self-love you are being of service.

Walk your talk — live, breathe and create love in all moments and watch the world change.

Below are some things to consider when being of service.

- Never be of service if it negatively impacts on your value — don't burden your life to help others. This is a very unloving thing to do to yourself.

- Never be of service with the intention of getting something back in return — no expectancy of self-gain. If you are thinking, *'What's in it for me?'* you miss the point of being of service.

- Always give with a pure intent to bring benefit to other aspects of yourself (that is, other people).

I have a sincere desire and intent to genuinely bring benefit to all life. I often sit and ponder, *'How can I be more effective in being of service?'* Pondering on this question/subject helps bring insights into better ways to be of service. Do your best to function from this purpose in every interaction with people. This is a loving way to be.

And most of all:

- **Be Humble**
- **Be Sincere**
- **Be Gracious**
- **Be Loving**
- **Be Truthful**
- **Be Honest**